NOW WE ARE SIXTY
(AND A BIT)

by a Member of the Public

NOW WE ARE SIXTY
(AND A BIT)
BY CHRISTOPHER MATTHEW
DECORATIONS BY DAVID ECCLES

JOHN MURRAY
London

For Wendy—
now I'm sixty-four

Text © Christopher Matthew 2003

Illustrations © David Eccles 2003
*(With sincere and affectionate tribute
to the genius of Ernest Shepard)*

First published in 2003
by John Murray (Publishers)
A division of Hodder Headline

13 15 17 19 20 18 16 14 12

A CIP catalogue record for this title is available from the British Library

ISBN 978-0-7195-6521-2

Typeset in Goudy Old Style
by Servis Filmsetting Limited, Manchester
Printed and bound in Great Britain by
Butler and Tanner Ltd, Frome and London

John Murray (Publishers)
338 Euston Road
London
NW1 3BH

INTRODUCTION

The great Bob Monkhouse was once asked on a television chat show if he was afraid of death. 'No,' he said, and paused. 'Mind you,' he went on, 'you don't half feel stiff the next morning.'

Faced with the fact that various bits of one's anatomy are, whether one likes it nor not, beginning to display embarrassing signs of wear and tear – what else is one to do but make light of it?

Hence this second volume of verses, inspired – like its predecessor – by A.A. Milne's familiar and well-loved poems for six-year-olds and adapted for those who are ten times older.

When *Now We Are Sixty* came out four years ago, I had no plans for penning a sequel. I felt I had made all the jokes I could and said all the things I thought needed saying about the ageing process.

But, then, towards the end of 2002, following a brisk skirmish with the surgeon's knife, I found myself toying with a few more poems – particularly ones based on originals that I hadn't tackled before, such as The Emperor's Rhyme and Sneezles.

P.G. Wodehouse once said about writing musical

comedies, 'It's a bit like eating salted almonds: you find you can manage just one more.' For musical comedies, read comic poems.

Before I knew what, a whole book's worth had been written.

As before, it celebrates the pleasures (and records some of the perils) of ageing, and confronts a wide variety of disconcerting problems that modern life throws our way.

I may give the impression of treating old age with the ridicule it deserves but, believe me, the air of insouciance conceals the same anxieties that beset all my contemporaries. I only hope these Milnesque divertissements may help to allay some of yours.

Like many of my friends, I am frequently reminded that I am within sight of the homeward stretch, but I don't have to believe it if I don't want to.

CONTENTS

GOLDEN DAYS
(*after* SOLITUDE)

I sit for hours on the grass
   On long summer afternoons.
I smile at girls as they pass,
   But they never see.
Some strip off, bold as brass—
It could be a Whitehall farce.
Sometimes I feel a right arse:
   But no one cares except me.

SIR JOHN'S FURTHER FANCY
(*after* KING JOHN'S CHRISTMAS)

Sir John was quite a vain man—
   He'd known his share of praise:
A knighthood and a CBE—
   He'd seen the best of days.
And great men when they spoke of him
   In boardrooms here and there
Would shake their heads and give a sigh,
And tap a nose and wink an eye,
And murmur, 'Ah, yes! What a guy!
   A man beyond compare!'

Sir John was quite a rich man—
   He had a place in Spain,
A chalet in St Moritz and
   A yacht called *Freckly Jane*.
He'd named it for his girlfriend;
   He'd hoped she'd be his wife—
His soulmate in his twilight years,
The envy of his golf club peers,
The one who'd calm his old-age fears,
   The true love of his life.

Sir John was not a mean man—
　　This view he'd oft express'd:
'Why bother with the second rate
　　When you can have the best?'
But though he gave her everything
　　A woman could desire,
And took her off to West End shows,
And bought her frocks and furbelows,
And daily sent a dark red rose,
　　Their love did not catch fire.

Sir John was quite a sad man—
　　He missed his Freckly Jane.
He yearned for love, but had no hope
　　Of finding it again.
He gave up jogging in the park,
　　And put on pounds galore.
He cared no more for outward looks,
Or seeing plays, or reading books,
Or keeping up with TV cooks,
　　As he had done of yore.

Sir John had one ambition—
    He longed to be a peer.
A scarlet robe with ermine trimmed
    Would crown a great career.
He lobbied all his cronies
    To put them in the know.
He said, 'I'm not a man who cares
For those who put on phoney airs,
Like certain friends of Tony Blair's—
    They know where they can go.

'But I *would* like an earldom
    With thousands of acres,
And lots of days' shooting
    With movers and shakers—
Armorial bearings
    With leopards and lions,
And a family motto
    To leave to my scions.
And oh! What I'd love, and I yearn for (touch
    wood)
Is a·place in the ranks of the great and good.'

Sir John was not a proud man—
    He rang up Freckly Jane
And talked a while of this and that—
    Of yachts, and snow, and Spain.

And then he cut straight to the chase
    And told her everything.
He said, 'I hope you'll understand—
I'm not a snob, I'm far from grand;
For me the future lies in land,
    And all that it can bring.'

She said, 'Oh bollocks, Johnnie.
    You must be off your head!
If I were you, I'd take a pill
    And spend a week in bed.
You've made your reputation;
    You don't need fancy names,
And people calling you "My Lord"—
It strikes a really bogus chord.
A peerage is the mere reward
    For playing silly games.'

'You *don't* need an earldom,
    With acres and acres,
And cold winter days
    Spent with fat moneymakers,
Who dine at The Ivy
    With people like Archer,
And swan off on Concorde
    On any departure.
But oh! What I'd love, and I pray for (touch wood)
Is to know that you've put your long life to some good.'

Sir John was now a chaste man—
　　He never spoke again
To any of his cronies.
　　He sold his place in Spain,
And gave up all his businesses
　　And went to live in Leeds,
And spent the last years of his life
Without the comfort of a wife,
Away from toil and tears and strife,
　　In charitable deeds.

THE MORAL OF THIS STORY
　　IS SURELY ALL TOO PLAIN:
　　　　DON'T WASTE YOUR TIME
　　　　WITH DAFT IDEAS.
　　　　JUST SPEAK TO
　　　　FRECKLY JANE.

IF ONLY
(*after* AT HOME)

I want a scorcher
(A Page Three scorcher);
I want a nymphette to come to tea with me.
I'd give her crumpets
(Toasted, buttery)
And chocolate Bath Olivers and Earl Grey tea.

I'd love a bimbo
(A dolly-bird, an eyeful);
The sort of bird I used to know at twenty-one.
But now I'm an old geezer
(With short sight and dentures),
I reckon I'd be happy with just anyone.

CLAPPED OUT
(*after* SNEEZLES)

Timothy's Mini
Was rusty
And crusty;
The big end was
Starting
To knock.
The clutch plate was slipping,
The brake wasn't gripping;
What once was a car
Was a crock.
He tinkered
And fiddled,
And then
Sort of diddled,
And twiddled
A couple
Of knobs.
He had a good feel
Round the back
Of each wheel,
And tested the thingummybobs.

He read through some booklets
On car care
And part wear
To find out what ought
To be done

With brake pads and linings,
And strange sorts of whinings,
And engines that rumble
When run.
They all said the same,
Viz – a car that's gone lame
Should be changed for a model that's new;
So he asked his wife, Sheila,
To ring up a dealer
And put out a feeler
Or two.
Said the man, 'If I feel
That the deal
Could be real,
Then of course we'll
Be talking "Go, go."
But a car that is rusty
And crusty
Not trusty—
That must be
A big no, no.'

So Tim in the end
Rang a friend
In Southend,
Who said *he'd* recommend
A chap
Who lived out near Brentwood—
'I daresay this gent would
Agree he could
Take it for scrap.'

    *   *

Timothy Binney
Got into his Mini
And drove fifty miles to the sea,
Where he smoked a cigar
And said, 'Farewell car,
All too soon this could happen to me!'

STINKER
(*after* BINKER)

Stinker—as I call him—is a one-off, that's for sure:
What my dear departed Dad would call 'a real
    plat du jour'.
If I'm sitting on the sofa, watching Countdown after tea,
Or doing the Times crossword, there'll be Stinker,
    on my knee.

    His father's quite a pleasant man, a funny looking
        bloke;
    He can be quite amusing—for a chap from
        Basingstoke.
    And Maggie—well, she's Maggie, and she mixes
        with strange folk . . .
                But they're not
                Like
                Stinker.

Stinker's quite obsessive, about slugs and snails and worms,
And centipedes and millipedes and anything that squirms.
He has a large collection which he keeps beside his bed,
And looks at it for hours and hours while standing
    on his head.

His father is a banker who makes millions every year,
And has his own collection, which includes a small Vermeer.
And Maggie—well, she's Maggie, and she's really
    very queer . . .
                    But they're not
                    Like
                    Stinker.

Stinker has ambitions to become an Argonaut,
Or an archer, like the ones who beat the French at Agincourt;
But his hero's an explorer by the name of Captain Oates.
'I'm going out . . .' etc. is a line he often quotes.

His father jets around the world, like Ariel gone mad;
He's known in every first-class lounge from JFK to Chad;
And Maggie—well, she's Maggie, a regular maenad . . .
                    But they're not
                    Like
                    Stinker.

Stinker is my grandson, and for me can do no wrong.
He's six years old and regularly beats me at mah-jong.
I don't say he's a genius, he cannot spell for nuts;
But he's my best companion now—no doubts, or ifs,
        or buts.

Look—I'm really fond of Maggie, but she's got no
   time for me;
And her husband's mostly forty thousand feet
   above the sea;
And my daily is a sweetie—when she isn't drinking
   tea . . .
But Stinker's always Stinker—though he's buggered
   up my knee.

SO, FAREWELL THEN . . .
(*after* CHERRY STONES)

Playboy, Rock Star,

Scientist, Frock Tsar,

Art Collector,

Ex-M.P.—

Captain of Industry,
Diplomat, Crooner,

Racehorse Trainer,
And Rich Grandee.

Don't forget the Law Lord, and the old Queen Mother;
The actress from that Hitchcock film—or do I mean
    another?

And the talented photographer who shot the great
    and good,
And the pianist from Dagenham who went to
    Hollywood.

And then there was that Mafia boss they nicknamed
    Joe Bananas,
And Claus, the German son-in-law of ex-Queen
    Juliana's . . .

Obituaries are not what you might call a cause for glee—
Unless, of course, the subjects are miles senior to me.

THE GOLFER WHO NEVER SHANKED
(*after* THE KNIGHT WHOSE ARMOUR DIDN'T SQUEAK)

Of all the golfers in the club
   The oldest was Sir Arthur Pratt.
For fifty years he'd been the hub
   Of spike bar chaff and smoke-room chat.
His name graced every honours board;
Of silverware he had a hoard.

His record was beyond compare
   For knock-out cups and foursomes won,
And monthly medals everywhere,
   And friendly rounds with everyone.
While others struggled in the gorse,
His ball stayed firmly on the course.

He never stamped or yelled or swore
    When putts went short or slipped on by.
But some things did stick in his craw
    And turn him into Captain Bligh—
Like snail's pace play of any kind
When he was coming up behind.

The chaps who most got up his nose
    Were those whose play was really bad,
With shots they struggled to compose
    As long as Homer's Iliad.
They'd swing the club and promptly duff
And smash the ball into the rough.

He didn't hook, he didn't slice,
  And very, very rarely missed
(Although he did so, maybe twice,
  One Boxing Day when he was pissed).
At Winkworth Golf Club he was ranked
The Member Who Had Never Shanked.

Sir Arthur was a little man
  With snow-white hair and pinkish hue,
Who looked as sweet as Peter Pan,
  But could turn into Fu Manchu,
And make those who provoked his wrath
Feel like a length of damp dishcloth.

One day Sir Arthur drove the first—
  Two hundred yards; the perfect lie—
Acknowledged the spontaneous burst
  Of warm applause from friends nearby;
Strolled to the ball, took out his three,
And shanked it straight into a tree.

His adversary—chap named Mick—
    Could not conceal his utter glee:
Said, 'Bad luck, Arthur. Makes you sick.
    I'll take a look, leave it to me.
The truth—if I may be so frank—
Is simply this: *all* golfers shank.'

But as Mick plunged into the rough,
    And brambles pricked and nettles stung,
Sir Arthur thought, 'I've had enough,'
    And dropped another ball and swung.
It hit the tree, the ground, a hut,
And bounced straight back and caught Mick's nut.

Now Mick, whose irons had never strayed,
  Has got the shanks—and serve him right.
One golden rule must be obeyed:
  You never cross a golfing knight.
Take heed the man who dares to snub
The oldest member of the club.

TOUCH AND GO
(*after* BROWNIE)

All around my bed is a great big curtain;
There's someone there behind it, but I don't know who.
It sounds to me like doctors, but I can't be certain,
And specialists and nurses, too.

They're talking very quietly and muttering together
About the need for surgery, or therapy, or what.
It all sounds pretty dodgy, and I don't know whether
I'm the subject of their little plot.

ALL AT SEA
(*after* THE OLD SAILOR)

There was once an old geezer who fancied a cruise
In the hope it would banish his post-Christmas
    blues.
But the brochures were so full of sun and
    champagne
That they jumbled his daydreams and addled his
    brain.

There were so many places he wanted to see—
From the frozen Antarctic to sunny Capri—
And the wider the choices of every kind,
The less he was able to make up his mind.

Should he snorkel with stingrays off Florida's
    Keys?
Or sail to Hawaii and suntan his knees?
Or broaden his outlook in classical Greece?
Or sample the seafood in Sydney, or Nice?

His long-suff'ring sister said, 'Give us a break;
It doesn't much matter which package you take.
They're all much the same, and the sea is the sea
In Jamaica, or Capetown, or Trincomalee.

'So stop all this fussing: go anywhere hot
That has palm trees and blue seas, and don't be a clot.
Throw off inhibitions and loosen your grip;
All life's an adventure, so let yourself rip.'

So he booked himself onto the Saga Princess,
In a junior suite, with a sea view, no less;
And for two solid weeks of Caribbean sun
He gave himself up to sheer pleasure and fun.

From first thing each morning till last thing at night
He was mildly, pleasantly, ever so tight.
He tried every cocktail (except the Gin Fizz),
And pitted his brains in the Musical Quiz.

And he threw himself into diversions galore,
From trap shoots to crap shoots and whist drives,
    and more.
At the Fancy Dress Evening he made quite a mark
In an up-turned ice bucket, as Otto Bismarck.

At the Island Night Dinner he made his best score
With a dazzling tribute to Dottie Lamour.
And to crown his great triumph he limbo-ed till dawn
With a well-endowed widow from Ealing, called Lorn.

The following morning he rose sharp at eight,
And brought her her breakfast in bed on a plate;
And that afternoon saw their new friendship bloom
With some brisk Indoor Games in the Carousel Room.

Next day during Deck Quoits he spoke to a man
Of about the same age, with a condo in Cannes.
'That woman in red has revived my sex drive.'
The man said, 'Good egg! I've already had five!'

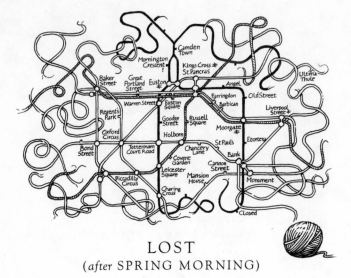

LOST
(*after* SPRING MORNING)

Where am I going? I don't quite know:
To Mornington Crescent? Or Bromley-by-Bow?
I said that I'd be at my daughter's at three,
And got on at Neasden as fit as a flea.

I got off the Jubilee just after two,
And thought I had changed to the old Bakerloo.
I was doing the crossword and feeling upbeat,
The next thing I knew, I'd reached Liverpool Street.

I jumped on the Central and went to the Bank,
The way to the District was crowded and dank.
I sat like a zombie, bereft of all thought;
Before I knew what, I'd arrived at Earl's Court.

For some silly reason I cannot explain,
I decided to hop on a Cockfosters train,
Not knowing an incident somewhere ahead
Near Holborn had turned all the signals to red.

What to do next? Well, the obvious thing
Was to contact my daughter—to give her a ring.
I was only at Knightsbridge; I'd walk to Sloane
    Square,
And change at Embankment—it's four stops from
    there . . .

I don't know what happened; I misread the sign,
And now I'm at Goodge Street on quite the wrong
    line.
Where am I going? St Pancras? King's Cross?
Well, the way things are looking, I don't give a toss.

WARDROBE
(*after* HAPPINESS)

John had
A pair
Of new suede
Shoes, and
John had a
Pair of
Bright green
Socks.
John couldn't
Reach be-
Yond his knees,
So they stayed
Where they
Were—in
The
Box.

WILLY'S WOBBLY
(*after* TEDDY BEAR)

A chap, however hard he tries,
Can lose desire, the more time flies.
Poor Willy Brown is off his oats,
Despite his wife on whom he dotes.
He thinks a lot about amour;
It always used to work before.
Just like a fine, well-oiled machine,
He'd follow the same old routine—
Put out his fag, put out the cat,
Put out the light, and after that,
Bound up the stairs—he couldn't wait
To satisfy his life's soulmate.

Then one day—bang!—out of the blue
It all goes wrong: he's in a stew.
It starts off fine, it's going well,
But when it matters—bloody hell!
The tower falls, the walls collapse;
His spirits slump; his courage snaps.
His wife enquires, 'What's this about?
The ruddy thing's just given out!
Is this a case of brewer's droop?'
He feels a perfect nincompoop.

Now impotence is just the thing
To get a fellow worrying.
In pubs, at work, and on the train,
He stares at everyone in vain,
And envies men who strut about
And tell crude jokes and drink and shout,
And thinks, 'There's no way *I* could fail
To be a real red-blooded male.
Am I alone of all my sex
To suffer from this fearful hex?'

He hears a talk on You and Yours
About the dread male menopause,
And wonders if he's reached 'that age',
And turned the corner, turned the page.
He thinks, 'Of course, I could be gay,'
And flies off to the USA.
He gives his greying hair a bleach,
And hurries down to Muscle Beach.
He pumps some iron, swings on bars,
(And thinks he spots two movie stars).

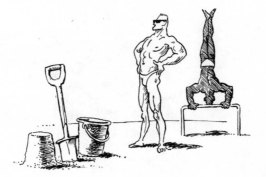

He tries his best to get some dates,
And buys a pair of roller skates.
He gets a tan and oils his pecs,
And even gives up wearing specs.
He talks the talk, swims in the swim,
But not one beach bum fancies him.
So back he crawls to Potters Bar—
His wife says, 'Willy, there you are!
That blooming boiler's on the blink,
And something's blocking up the sink . . .'

That night he supplements his gloom
By moving to the single room.
He lies awake for several hours,
Despite three pills and two hot showers.
He slips downstairs at half past three
And makes himself a pot of tea;
And, like Achilles in his tent,
He gives a sigh, all passion spent,
And wonders if there's anything
That might restore his erstwhile zing.

Next thing he knows, his wife is there,
Her curlers bristling in her hair.
She says, 'You really *are* the end;
At this rate you'll go round the bend.
You're sixty-three, for heaven's sake,
Not Rudolph Valentino's Sheik.
Your waistline looks like baker's dough;
Your body's on one big go-slow.
Forget about your limp sex drive;
You're lucky to be still alive.

And don't forget the golden rule—
There's no fool like an ageing fool.
So do stop fussing, come to bed
And think about your wife instead.
A few soft words, a gentle kiss,
A cuddle, that's my kind of bliss.
And as for getting back your zip—
What *you* need is a good night's kip.'

A chap, however hard he tries,
Can lose desire, the more time flies.
No man can re-discover youth—
That is a universal truth;
And Willy's had a marvellous life,
With marvellous kids and marvellous wife,
And health and all that that can bring—
So there: you can't have everything.

DISABLED
(*after* IN THE FASHION)

My neighbour's got a permit for his dodgy back,
And so has my cousin for her heart attack,
And I need a hip-job—or so says the quack,
But *I* have to park where I can.

For two pins I'd pop round to Kall Kwik and fake
one;
It surely can't take rocket science to make one.
Or shall I just nip to my cousin's and take one?
That sounds like a very good plan.

Then I'd park in a space marked 'DISABLED' each
day,
And swan round the shops and drink café au lait,
And smile at the warden and be on my way,
And, by golly, I'd feel twice the man.

TOGETHERNESS
(*after* US TWO)

Wherever I am, there's always You,
There's always You and Me.
Whatever I do, you want to do:
'Where are you off to today?' say you.
'I'm going to visit some friends in Kew.'
'Well, oddly enough,' you say to me,
'I'm heading out that way, too.'

'What's on the box?' I say to you.
'Commercial or BBC?'
'I rather fancy something blue
On Channel 5 at half past two.'
'Oh good, I'm all for something new.
It makes a change from ITV—
A cultural debut.'

'Let's take a trip to Timbuktu.'
'Yes, let's,' you say to me.
'Or study herds of caribou,
Or backpack off to Katmandu,
Or dive for pearls in Tuvalu.'
You say, 'I'd live in old Torquay—
It's really up to you.'

'Let's go quite mad,' I say to you.
'Why not?' you say to me.
'We'll diddle the Inland Revenue,
We'll blow up the Palace and set off a coup,
And rob a few banks and not leave a clue.'
'I'm right behind you,' you say with glee,
'I'm all for a switcheroo.'

So wherever I am, there's always You,
There's always You and Me.
Whatever I do, you silly old moo—
If I married another, you'd be there, too.
Like Gilbert and George we're as solid as glue.
There are times, I admit, when I long to be free,
But it's much more fun with Two.

WALKIES
(*after* DISOBEDIENCE)

Bob, Ben,
Treacle and Doormat,
Daisy and Mollie and Gyp
Loved their
Walkies with Archie,
Though it gave him the pip.
Bob, Ben,
Daisy and Treacle,
Mollie and Doormat and Gyp
Did plenty of barking and chasing and larking,
    until he fair lost his grip.

One day
Archie Macdonald
Tripped on a tuft of grass—
Lost his
Balance completely,
Came down hard on his arse.
Lay there puffing and groaning,
Turned to the faithful Gyp
And said 'Well I never, that's not very clever—
    I've buggered my stupid hip.'

The quack
Waggled his finger—
Read him the riot act:
'You are
Really quite lucky,
Your femur is only crack'd.
These things
Heal pretty quickly;
Meanwhile, if I were you,
I'd sit on my backside, take life on the slack side—
    that's my professional view.'

Poor old
Archie Macdonald
(Known to his friends as Mac)
Rang his
Next door neighbour—
Fat little fellow called Jack.
'Can you
Do me a favour?
Take all my dogs to the park—
They just need a piddle and run round the middle
    and generally have a good bark.'

Bob, Ben,
Treacle and Doormat
Caused a most frightful ruck:
Daisy
Chased a few squirrels;
Gyp tried to roger a duck.
Archie
Wrote out a notice;
Jack stuck it up on a tree:
'FOR SALE: A COLLECTION
OF MUTTS. FOR INSPECTION,
RING 245 873.'

*(To be spoken in a soft, low, sympathetic voice—except
for the last line)*

B, B,
T, D,
D, M & G
Went to new homes in Esher,
Just off the old A3.
Archie
Bought a black moggie;
Said to fat Jack, 'If we
Have learnt one thing from this: inactivity's bliss.
    I'm as happy as happy can be.'

UNIMPRESSED
(*after* VESPERS)

Little man sits up alone in his bed;
Pulls at his ear-lobe, scratches his head—
'Well, well, what do you know . . . ?'
Roddy Scott-Johnstone is reading Hello!

'Who *are* these people—I haven't a clue—
With their suntans and fun plans and
      champagne *grand cru*?
If they're not getting married, or throwing a bash,
They've some other reason for being right flash.

'That chap's a film star—I know that's right;
And didn't I see her on telly last night?
Or is she the one who is married to Thing—
The one who's a pop star but simply can't sing?

'And who is this pair with their "riverside home",
And their sofas and curtains in pink monochrome,
And their hair all pouffed up like a lacquered
　　　meringue,
And their friends who look just like the Al Capone
　　　gang?

'I suppose I should know each celebrity's name,
And be versed in the mysteries of modern-day
　　　fame.
But to tell you the truth, I'm too bored and too
　　　old,
And I couldn't care less even if I was told.'

Little man stretches out flat in his bed;
Closes his eyes tight and lays down his head:
Yawns, sighs, 'Don't want to know.'
Roddy Scott-Johnstone has binned his Hello!

HOME
(after THE WRONG HOUSE)

They took me to this house, this very nice house,
     With nice front steps and a nice big hall.
'This is where you live now,
          Mummy,'
          They told me.
But it isn't *my* house at all.

They took me round the garden, this nice big garden,
     With nice bright borders and a high brick wall.
'This is where you walk now,
          Mummy,'
          They told me.
But it isn't *my* garden at all.

They took me to a bedroom, this nice big bedroom,
   With a nice colour telly and prints on the wall.
'This is where you sleep now,
      Mummy,'
      They told me.
But it isn't *my* bedroom at all.

They took me to a lounge, this nice sunny lounge,
   Full of old dears who said nothing at all.
'These are your friends now,
      Mummy,'
      They told me.
But they're not *my* friends at all.

They got into their car, their nice big car,
   And they waved goodbye just before nightfall . . .
'This is your life now,
      Betty,'
      I murmured.
But it isn't *my* life at all.

CHAIRS
(*after* NURSERY CHAIRS)

One of the chairs is reserved for the chairman;
One's being kept for the next M.D.;
One is reserved for the Finance Director;
And one (I hope) is for me!

First Plan
When I go up on the seven-o-one
With the chaps from the firm, we have great fun.
    We scan the old FT
To check the latest interest rates
And how the market fluctuates
    And where our funds should be.
And when we've filled in 3 Across
And made some jokes about the boss,
    To universal glee,
We grab a cab at Charing Cross
    And head for Potters Quay.

I'm the top fund manager at Pinchbecks—
　　To be frank, I'm a pretty big cheese;
　　I'm a whizz with unit trusts, and
　　I have got some plans for Dockland.
So everything is going like a breeze.

Second Plan

When I am Chairman, or M.D.,
   I'll launch a really hostile bid
For Barclays or the TSB,
   And match my rivals quid for quid.
And when they say, 'He's off his tree,'
   I'll do what all those big boys did,
And hit them with a left and right
   That no one could foresee . . .

Actual Plan

I thought it was all hunky-dory,
   And I felt a most wonderful glow.
Then they said they were terribly sorry;
   They were having to let me go.

I'm thinking of turning consultant,
  Or living in Paris, or Rome;
But at sixty does anyone want me?
  I might as well sit here at home.

THINGY
(*after* FORGIVEN)

They've found a little tumour; carcinoma is its name,
And I call it 'Little Thingy', which is more or less the
    same.
It's sitting in my prostate and it's been there for a year.
    The surgeon wants my thingy out—
        He wants to take my thingy out—
           And give me the all-clear.

He says it isn't urgent; it can wait a month or two,
Or three or four or even more—I'll want to think it
    through.
He says he's very sorry, though not half as much as me.
The stupid thing about it is, I never need to pee.

I know some blokes about my age who seem to be all
    right,
But, when it comes to widdling, are at it half the night.
I haven't any problems—my widdle rate is low—
I'll sit through half of Parsifal and still not need to go.

I can't think what came over me; I must be off my head.
'If it ain't broke don't mend it' is what I've always said.
I went to see my doctor, who is something of a chum;
The next thing that I knew he'd got his finger up my
    bum.

'We'd best be on the safe side, and just check your
    PSA.
I'll need to take a drop of blood—I do it every day.
The chances are it's normal; I would really be amazed
To find a fit young chap like you whose PSA was
    raised . . .'

Well—now I've got this thingy; I could have it till I croak.
Mind you, the old Grim Reaper is a tricky sort of bloke.
The question one must ask oneself is this—in simple
    terms—
Does one leave sleeping dogs asleep—or risk a can of
    worms?

EATING
(*after* A THOUGHT)

If tea were lunch and lunch were tea,
I'd eat roast beef at half past three.
If lunch were tea and tea were lunch,
I frankly wouldn't care a bunch.

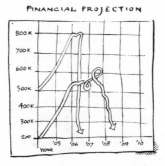

FINANCIAL PROJECTION

CRYSTAL BALLS
(*after* JONATHAN JO)

Wouldn't you know—
My statement reads 'O',
Despite countless years of investment.
I've bought ISAs and PEPs
From smooth-talking reps
Who have offered financial assessment.

I've ploughed thousands of pounds
   (On the soundest of grounds)
Into stakeholder pensions and things,
   And various schemes,
     Which provide—so it seems—
The comfort that far-thinking brings.

I've tried *not* to sound smug,
  Or be seeming to plug
Peace of mind to my less prudent chums—
  Which is all just as well,
  Because now—bloody hell!—
They're the ones sitting smug on their bums.

SPOILT
(*after* KING HILARY AND THE
BEGGARMAN)

Of Ernestine, the Short and Stout
   (or Lady Grundy, should I say,
A woman of enormous clout
And wealth and influence, no doubt,
But basically a dull old trout)
   They say that, one fine day,
She threw away her life of bliss—
The story goes a bit like this:

Old Lady Grundy
Said to her companion
(Dorothy from Dorking,
Forty-five and mousey),
'Open the window,
There's a good girl,
Quickly, quickly,
   And see who is calling.

It may be the postman,
Dusky, mysterious,
Bringing me offers,
Scratch cards and circulars.
It may be the milkman,
Crinkle-eyed and saucy,
Bringing me orange juice
    And something enthralling.'

Dorothy from Dorking,
Dowdy and put-upon,
    Cursed her under her breath.
'I've worked for you, you silly old bat,
For five long years, or more than that,
But you still behave like a spoiled little brat.
    You're worse than Lady Macbeth.'

Old Lady Grundy
Snapped at her companion
(Sad little Dorothy,
Spinsterish and hang-dog),
'Answer the telephone,
Don't just stand there,
Hurry, hurry,
   And see who is ringing.
It may be Wogan,
Tanned and twinkly,
Asking me to join him
At Claridges for tea.
It may be Edinburgh,
Mischievous as always,
Saying would I fancy
   Some ring-a-ding-dinging?'

Poor little Dorothy
Smiled at her ladyship;
   Thought, 'You lump of fat—
I've pandered like a fool to your every need,
And I've turned a blind eye to your sickening greed,
And I've wormed your chihuahua twice yearly—indeed
   I have greased the boil on your cat.'

Old Lady Grundy
Said to her companion
(Dreary little Dorothy,
Grim-faced and care-worn),
'Answer the front door,
Get your skates on,
Quickly, quickly,
   And see who is knocking.

It may be Connery,
Seventy but sexy,
Bringing me martinis—
Gin, not vodka.
It may be Jeremy,
Pressing me for answers,
Telling me to hurry up,
    And trying to be shocking.'

Funny little Dorothy
Pulled on her cardigan;
    Said, 'I've had enough.
You treat me like a dirty rag,
My life with you is one long drag,
You're nothing but a sad old bag;
    It's my turn to play rough.'

Dear, kind Dorothy
Looked at her employer
(Outsize Ernestine,
Pop-eyed and powdered).
She thumbed her nose
At the silly, fat frog-face,
And ran to the front door,
    All of a fluster.
It wasn't Sean Connery,
Or Wogan, or Edinburgh,
It wasn't old Paxman,
Barking bossily,
Or even the milkman
Saying ''allo, darling',
But only an immigrant
    Selling her a duster.

73

Wide-eyed Dorothy
Gazed at the immigrant,
   And beamed with new-found glee.
She looked the poor man up and down:
'Your hair's too long and your skin's too brown,
You're not very tall and you look like a clown.
   So what? You'll do for me!'

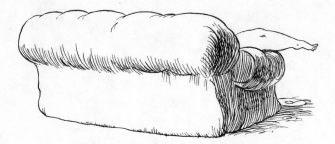

Of Ernestine the stout (and short),
There's little news. Her friends report
She lies upon the davenport
   Completely in the nude,
And rings the local takeaway
At any hour of night or day,
And orders breakfast on a tray
   In language somewhat rude.

While Dorothy, so I've heard tell,
Now manages a small hotel,
And lives in sin in Camberwell
   In blessed quietude.

BREATHER
(*after* HALFWAY DOWN)

Halfway up the stairs
Is a spot
Where I sit.
I feel a really
Stupid clot—
A silly old
Twit.

I'm not some poor cripple
With only one leg.
I've got all my limbs—
I'm
A tough old
Egg.

I haven't had a stroke,
And I'm not
The least gaga,
Or suff'ring from angina,
Just like my dear papa.
But when you get to my age
Of sixty-five or more,
And travel to
Australia,
You stop in Singa-
pore.

DISGUISE
(*after* FURRY BEAR)

If I had some hair
   Where my hair once grew,
I wouldn't much care
   If a Force Six blew,
Or I dived in the Med
   In the South of France,
Or a pretty girl said,
   'D'you want to dance?'

But I wear a rug. It's a kind of a wig—
A touch Liberace, though not so big.
It's meant to look just like a natural thatch,
And fit like a glove in a wonderful match.
But, try as I might, I'm a man with a toup,
And one of these days it'll fall in the soup.

INSTRUCTIONS
(*after* SPRING MORNING)

What *am* I doing? I really don't know,
Kneeling in front of this damned video.
I want to record the Jane Austen at eight—
I'd have better luck teaching a lobster to skate.

My children can work it, and so can their lot,
And so can my husband, and he's a real clot.
Oh why did he have to go bowling tonight?
Did he leave me in charge of this thing out of spite?

I've read the instructions again and again,
But they might as well be an advanced class in Zen.
The last time I tried to tape Top Gear on Two,
We found ourselves watching a thing on the Zoo.

'Page 10. MANUAL TIMING. Turn On the TV.
Press Menu. Then Manual.' And then one *should*
    see
A list of six choices. If I press OK,
It should take me to TUNING. Or is that
    DISPLAY?

Oh no! I've just realised: I'm on the wrong page.
I want TIME RECORDING—it must be my age.
'Insert a cassette.' No, I've done that before.
'Press PROG/CHECK'—oh why does it say
　　Channel 4?

I've pressed a few arrows and made a right muck,
And I've started again and I've still had no luck,
And I've turned the thing off and I've stared at the
　　walls—
I give up! In the words of Miss Austen, 'Oh *balls!*'

INCONTINENCE
(*after* HOPPITY)

Buster McMaster goes
Widdly, widdly,
Widdly, widdly, wee.
Whenever he nips off
To have a quick piddle, he
Piddles all over his knee.

He shakes it about like a bloke in Caracas,
Who plays in a band
With a pair of maracas . . .
But still he goes widdly,
Widdly, widdly,
Widdly,
Widdly,
Wee.

ASKING FOR IT
(*after* RICE PUDDING)

What is the matter with everyone?
I've never been rude and I've never been snide,
Or behaved like a man who's been certified,
Yet you'd think I'm Attila the Hun.

Whatever became of good manners and charm?
Today I got bumped from an Underground queue
Just for saying I'd never seen so many who
Behaved like the pigs on a farm.

I parked for a second last week on a line,
And nipped into Waitrose to pick up some bread,
And picked up a £40 ticket instead.
The warden *deserved* the word 'swine.'

I ordered a coffee, and so did my friend—
The waiter poured most of it into my lap
When I murmured, 'He looks like the kind of a chap
Who bowls from the Nursery End.'

I ticked off a youth who was having great fun
On the top of a bus, flicking pieces of pie.
The next thing I knew he'd spat all down my tie.
What *is* the matter with everyone?

I WISH
(*after* IF I WERE KING)

I often wish that I were dead,
Instead of lying here in bed,

And torturing my silly head
With everything from A to Zed:

With germs and poisons being spread,
And all that blood so freely shed,

And why we're all so badly led,
And who should do the job instead,

And what it was my wife once said
About what's in the garden shed,

And what became of poor old Ted,
And, while I think about it, Fred,

And why I am not better read,
And should I move to Leatherhead?

I often wish that I were dead,
And free from mortal fear and dread.

But here I am, tucked up in bed,
Hanging by a tiny thread.

STRICTLY BALLROOM
(*after* MARKET SQUARE)

I learnt to mambo,
And rumba and tango,
And dance the fandango
Along with the best.
I wanted to meet a
Nice plump señorita—
Perhaps called Conchita—
With fire in her breast.

So I went to a place where they held *thés dansants*
(*All nice people; all bien pensants*):
'Can anyone tango—not any old nonsense?'
  But no one did the tango; *what* a fruitless quest!

I learnt the Eightsome,
The Dashing White Sergeant,
The old Gay Gordons,
And the Highland Fling.
I fancied some reeling
With someone appealing
In Acton, or Ealing,
Or, failing that, Tring.

So I went to a do where they said there'd be dancing
(*What better way for a spot of romancing?*):
'Anyone up for some jigging and prancing?'
But no one cried, 'Hoots, mon!'—or said anything.

I learnt to foxtrot
My footwork is v. hot;
I've got what Fred's got—
Call me Astaire.
With top hat and white tie
And tails, I'm a swell guy;
I could fly sky high
And float on air.

So I put on my glad rags and went to the Palais
(*Nothing like a dance hall for getting quite pally*):
'Anyone for foxtrot? Don't dilly-dally.'
   But not a single person even looked at me, I
     swear.

I hate ballroom;
For me it's just all gloom.
I gave my costumes
To a charity shop.
Now I've met this hippie
Who's lippy and dippy,
But keeps me pretty zippy
On the disco floor.

So I'm sorry for the trippers of the light fandango;
I'm sorry for the devotees of Fred and Ginger;
I'm sorry for the kilted laddies and lassies;
   'Cos they make you feel about as young as
     Zsa Zsa Gabor.

AIDES MEMOIRES
(*after* THE EMPEROR'S RHYME)

A chap's got to do
What a chap's got to do
    When he's feeling his age
      At about eight-five;
And his blood's getting thin,
So his head's in a spin,
    And he's got to a stage
      When he's lacking in drive . . .

And his bowels are a joke,
And they need a de-coke,
    And he suffers dejection
        From coffee and tea;
And develops a rash
Like the worst pebble dash,
    Plus a nasty infection
        He caught in Dundee . . .

Oh whenever a wrinkly
Loses his twinkle he
    Rattles with tablets galore,
Which he swallows by rote
As per this little note,
    Stuck up on the freezer door:

Three white at breakfast time,
    A red one at eleven;
After lunch
Be sure to munch
    A garlic pill from Devon.
Two green with every meal,
    And don't forget this coda:
Before you sleep
Take one small heap
    Of carbonate of soda.

When a chap's in a stew,
Just like me—or like you—
    So he cannot bend down
        Just to pull on a sock;
And he sits on his bed
With its crumpled bedspread,
    Like a Bertram Mills clown
        In a broken-down crock;

And he utters a groan
In a low monotone
    When he stretches an arm
      For a cup on a shelf;
And he ends up in pain
When he runs for a train;
    Though he tries to stay calm
      He fair knackers himself . . .

Oh whenever a wrinkly
Loses his twinkle he
    Does some aerobics each day,
Which he learnt from a book
And, because he can't look,
    He has memorized, so he can say:

Twist trunk to left and right,
    Fifteen times or more;
Stretch each arm,
Like a salaam,
    Then do it on the floor.
Knees bend and straighten up
    Twenty times, and then,
When that's done,
Have a bun,
    And do it all again.

LUVVIES
(*after* TWICE TIMES)

There was an old couple who lived in a home—
Her name was Patricia and his was Jerome.
Pat was a sweetie to one and all,
But Jerry just sat with his hat in the hall.

They'd been on the stage in the good old days
In terrible reps in some terrible plays.
Jerry walked on as a priest in The Bells,
But Pat starred in Showboat in Tunbridge Wells.

They were stalwarts in movies just after the war
With Guinness and Hawkins—and dear Kenny More.
Jerry was shot down in Reach for the Sky,
But Pat made her mark in Where No Vultures Fly.

They broke into telly in '72
With a nice little sitcom called Just Me and You.
Jerry was cast as a plumber called Sam,
But Pat played the lead as a comic grande dame.

They gave up the business and lived by the sea
In a home for old actors in sunny Torquay.
Jerry turned into a thespian bore,
With stories of Wolfit—and dear Kenny More.

But Pat never mentioned her days on the boards,
Or her triumphs at Pinewood, or Bafta awards.
Jerry played Hamlet at Ilfracombe,
But Pat was the star in the morning room.

The moral, old darling, if moral there be,
Is that some of us get to the top of the tree,
And some of us struggle down here on the ground,
And keep being thrown off the merry-go-round.
The fact of the matter—and you may well scoff—
Is that life's an illusion—both on stage and off.

WHO WOULD HAVE GUESSED?
(*after* THE MORNING WALK)

When Jill and I were twenty-eight,
We'd lie in bed and contemplate
A life of endless joy and bliss,
And cuddle up, and hug, and kiss.

I never thought the day would come
When I'd be stuck here on my bum,
And baby Amy's first 'Ga ga'
Would best describe her grandmama.

WIND
(*after* WIND ON THE HILL)

Can anyone tell me?
  Does anyone know?
Where does wind come from
  Down there below?

I go to a concert
  Of Bach or Mozart—
Up goes the baton,
  Out comes a fart.

I'm waiting at Heathrow
  En route to Belfast—
Bend down for my luggage,
  And let off a blast.

I'm playing a bridge hand—
    The usual stuff—
I bid seven diamonds,
    And suddenly guff.

I'm sitting at dinner
    With stylish aplomb—
I sneeze: the result is
    A hydrogen bomb.

Can anyone tell me?
    Does anyone know?
Where does wind come from?
    And where *does* it go?

NODDING
(*after* KNIGHT-IN-ARMOUR)

If I have had a sleepless night
From restless legs, or being tight,
I sit around and feel quite odd,
As if I were some other bod.
And then I find some jobs to do—
Like polishing the downstairs loo,
And re-arranging magazines,
And cutting ends off runner beans . . .
And then I turn the telly on,
And close my eyes, and – phtt! – I'm gone.

FIRST IMPRESSIONS
(*after* THE FRIEND)

I met this bunch of hooligans with rings and studs
    and hair
All spiky as a bog brush. I thought 'Aye, aye . . .
    beware!'
I ducked my head and scuttled to the far side of the
    street—
Like Bonaparte in Russia, I know when to retreat.

'Don't look at them,' I told myself. 'Try not to
    catch their eye.
Remember, keep your head down, and with luck
    they'll walk on by.'
Then one of them crossed over, and things were
    looking bad;
And, as I closed my eyes in prayer, a voice said,
    'Hallo, Dad!'

STANDING ON THE PAVEMENT
(*after* WAITING AT THE WINDOW)

Bob and Geoff are two old farts
With shaky legs and dicky hearts.

While others gaily come and go,
They worry about traffic flow;

And, certain that the end is near
In busy, downtown Haslemere,

They stand there, like the Wife of Lot,
Rooted, rocklike, to the spot,

On either side, just down from Boots,
Mesmerised by beeps and hoots.

One day in winter, petrified,
They gaze across the great divide—

Should they wait or should they scram,
And risk becoming strawberry jam?

Bob decides to take the plunge,
Geoffrey's legs have turned to sponge.

Now it's Geoff who makes his play,
Then both of them are under way.

They dare not pause or look ahead,
But eyes a-swivel, filled with dread,

They beetle on, as cars and vans,
With blaring horns and waving hands,

And well-tuned brakes and squealing tyres,
Frustrate the waiting heavenly choirs.

Thus, dodging death on either side,
Halfway across, the pair collide.

And measuring their length, they shout:
'You silly prat!' 'You stupid lout!'

'You blind or something?' 'Learn to walk!'
'You need a wheelchair!' 'You should talk!'

They might as well just save their breath,
And settle for an early death.

THE BEGINNING
(*after* THE END)

At sixty-one
I had too much sun.

At sixty-two
I had dreadful 'flu.

At sixty-three
I couldn't pee.

At sixty-four
I felt really poor.

At sixty-five
I took a dive.

But at sixty-six, to be perfectly frank,
I'm as fit and as strong as a Sherman tank.